FRENCH
FIRST
NAMES

HIPPOCRENE BOOKS
New York

*A good name is rather to be chosen
than great riches.*
—PROVERBS 22:1

Contents

Girls' Names

Abélia
From Hebrew, meaning 'breath.'
Variant: Abella.

Ada
From Hebrew, meaning 'ornament.'
Variant: Adnette

❦ ❦ ❦

Adèle
From German, meaning 'noble.'
Variants: Adelaide, Adelaïde, Adélie, Adelina, Adeline, Aline.
Famous bearer of the name: Adèle Issac,
French soprano (1854–1915).

Adrienne
From Latin, meaning 'from the Adria' or 'from the Adriatic sea.'
Famous bearer of the name: Adrienne Rich,
American poet and essayist (born 1929).

❧ ❧ ❧

Agathe
From Greek, meaning 'good.'

❧ ❧ ❧

Agnès
From Greek, meaning 'pure' or 'chaste.'
Variant: Agneta, Agnete.
Famous bearer of the name: Agnès Varda,
French movie director (born 1928).

❧ ❧ ❧

Aimée
From French, meaning 'loved.'

❧ ❧ ❧

Albane
From Latin, meaning 'from the town of Alba.'

❧ ❧ ❧

Alberta
From German, meaning 'illustrious.'
Variants: Alberte, Albertine.

Alexandrine
From Greek, meaning 'defender of men.'

Alice
From German, meaning 'nobility.'
Variant: Aliette.
Famous bearer of the name: Alice Walker,
American author and poet (born 1944).

Alix
From German, meaning 'noble,' or used as a
diminutive of Alexandra.
Variants: Alexia, Alexiane.

Alphonsine
From German, meaning 'ready to combat.'

Amanda
From Latin, meaning 'lovable' or 'worthy of love.'
Variant: Amandine.
Famous bearer of the name: Amandine Aurore Lucie Dupin,
Baronne Dudevant (pseudonym: George Sand),
French novelist (1804–1876).

Amélie

From Latin, meaning 'from the Roman clan of the Emilius.'
Variants: Amelia, Ameline.
Famous bearer of the name: Amelia Earhart,
American aviator (1898–1937).

❖ ❖ ❖

Andrée

The feminine form of André.
From Greek, meaning 'man' or 'manly.'

❖ ❖ ❖

Angèle

The French form of Angela. From Greek, meaning 'angel' or
'divine messenger.'
Variants: Ange, Angélina, Angéline, Angelon.

❖ ❖ ❖

Angélique

From Latin, meaning 'like an angel.'
Variant: Angélica.
Famous bearer of the name: Angélique Arnaud,
French female priest from Port-Royal (1595–1661).

❖ ❖ ❖

Anne

From Hebrew, meaning 'grace.'
Variants: Anna, Annequin, Annette, Annick, Annie, Anita, Anny.
Famous bearers of the name: Anne Hébert, French-Canadian
poet (born 1916); Annie Girardot, French actress (born 1931).

Antoinette

From Latin, meaning 'from the Roman clan of the Antonius.'
Variant: Antonienne.
Famous bearer of the name: Marie-Antoinette,
queen of France (1755–1793).

Apolline

From Greek, meaning 'of Apollo, the Greek and Roman God of
sunlight, prophecy, music, and poetry.'

Ariane

From Greek, meaning 'very holy.'
Famous bearer of the name: Ariane Mnouchkine,
French motion-picture director (born 1939).

Arlette

From German, meaning 'strong' or 'courageous.'
Variants: Arlène, Arletty, Arline, Harlette.
Famous bearer of the name: Arlette-Léonie Bathiat
(pseudonym: Arletty), French actress (1898–1992).

Armelle

From Celtic, meaning 'princess of the bears.'
Variant: Armeline.

Aude

From German, meaning 'old territory.'
Variants: Audette, Audie.

Augustine

From Latin, meaning 'venerable.'
Variant: Augusta.
Famous bearer of the name: Augustine Brohan,
French actress of the Comédie Française Theater (1824–1893).

Aurélie

From Latin, meaning 'of the color of gold' or 'beautiful, lovely.'
Variants: Aure, Aurèle, Aurélia.

Aurore

From Latin, meaning 'dawn.'

Barberine
From Latin, meaning 'foreign.'
Variant: Barbe.

Béatrice
From Latin, meaning 'who makes happy' or
'who carries happiness.'
Variant: Béatrix.
Famous bearer of the name: Béatrice Lillie,
British comic actor (1898–1989).

Bénédicte
From Latin, meaning 'protected or blessed by God.'

Bérengère
From German, a combination of the words 'bear' and 'spear.'
Alternative spelling: Bérangère.
Famous bearer of the name: Bérengère de Navarre,
wife of Richard the Lion-Hearted (1165–1230).

Bernadette
From German, meaning 'courageous bear.'
Variant: Bernarde.
Famous bearer of the name: Bernadette Soubirus,
French peasant girl in Lourdes who was canonized by the
Catholic church and became St. Bernadette (1844–1879).

Berthe
From German, meaning 'bright.'
Variant: Bertille.

Bienvenue
From French, meaning 'welcome.'

Blanche
From French, meaning 'white.'

Blandine
From Latin, meaning 'charming.'

Brigitte
From Celtic, a combination of 'the high one' and 'strength.'
Famous bearer of the name: Brigitte Bardot,
French actress (born 1934).

ℭ

Camille
From Latin, name borne by servants of
certain priests in ancient Rome.
Variant: Cammie.
Famous bearer of the name: Camille Claudel,
French sculptor (1864–1943).

Carine
From Italian, meaning 'beloved.'

Carole
From German, meaning 'strong' or 'courageous.'
Variant: Caroline, Coralie.
Famous bearer of the name: Carole Lombard,
American actress (1908–1942); Carole Laure,
French-Canadian actress (born 1948).

Catherine
From Greek, meaning 'always pure.'
Variant: Cathie.
Famous bearer of the name: Catherine Deneuve,
French actress (born 1943).

Cécile
From Latin, meaning 'from the Roman clan of the Caecilius.'

Célestine
From Latin, meaning 'celestial.'
Variant: Célestina.

Céline
From Latin, probably meaning 'sky' or 'heaven.'
Variants: Célia, Célina, Linette.
Famous bearer of the name: Céline Dion,
French-Canadian singer (born 1968).

Césarine
From Latin, meaning 'from the Roman clan of
Gaius Julius Caesar.'

Chantal
From Occitan, meaning 'big, large stone.'
Famous bearer of the name: Chantal Akerman,
Belgian movie director (born 1950).

Charlotte
From German, meaning 'courageous.'
Famous bearer of the name: Charlotte Saunders Cushman,
American actress (1816–1876); Charlotte Gainsbourg,
French actress (born 1972).

Chloé
From Greek, meaning 'small green shoot of a plant.'
Famous bearer of the name: Chloe Anthony Wofford
(pseudonym: Toni Morrison), American novelist (born 1931).

❧ ❧ ❧

Christine
From Greek, meaning 'disciple of Christ.'
Variants: Christelle, Christiane.
Famous bearer of the name: Christine princess of France,
daughter of Henry IV and Marie de Médicis (1606–1663);
Christine de Pisan, French poet (1364–1430).

❧ ❧ ❧

Claire
From Latin, meaning 'clear.'
Variants: Clara, Clarisse, Clairette.

Claude
From Latin, meaning 'lame.'
Variants: Claudette, Claudie, Claudine.
Famous bearer of the name: Claudette Colbert,
French actress (1905–1996).

Clémence
From Latin, meaning 'mild' or 'merciful.'
Variant: Clémentine.

Clotilde
From German, combination of 'loud' or 'famous' and 'battle.'

Colombe
From Latin, meaning 'pigeon.'

Constance
From Latin, meaning 'firm.'
Variant: Constante.

Cora
From Greek, meaning 'girl.'
Variant: Coralie, Corinne.

Corentine
From Celtic, probably derived from 'raven.'

Danielle
From Hebrew, meaning 'God is the (only) judge.'
Variant: Danièle.

Daphné
From Greek, meaning 'laurel.'
Famous bearer of the name: Daphne du Maurier,
English novelist and short-story writer (1907–1989).

Déborah
From Hebrew, meaning 'bee.'
Famous bearer of the name: Deborah Butterfield,
American artist (born 1949).

Delphine
From Greek, meaning 'little sister.'
Variant: Dauphine.
Famous bearer of the name: Delphine Seyrig,
French actress (1932–1990).

Denise

From Greek, meaning 'sacred to Dionysos,
the God of wine and fertile crops.'
Alternative spellings: Denyse, Dennise.
Famous bearer of the name: Denise Scott-Brown, African-born
American urban planner and architect (born 1931).

Désirée

From Latin, meaning 'wished-for.'

Diane

From Latin, meaning 'goddess of fertility,
hunting and the moon.'
Variant: Dianna.
Famous bearer of the name: Diane Keaton,
American actress (born 1946).

Dominique

From Latin, meaning 'someone who belongs to God.'
Variant: Dominica.
Famous bearer of the name: Dominique Sanda,
French actress (born 1951).

Donatienne
From Latin, meaning 'given.'

Dorothée
From Greek, meaning 'gift from God.'

Edith

From German, combination of 'rich' and 'war.'
Famous bearer of the name: Edith Piaf,
French singer (1915–1963).

Edmonde

From German, meaning 'protector of wealth.'
Variant: Aymone.

Edouardine

From Old English, a combination of 'rich' and 'guardian.'

Edwige

From German, meaning 'refuge in war.'
Alternative spellings: Edwidge, Hedwige.
Famous bearer of the name: Edwidge Darticant,
Haitian-American writer (born 1969).

❖ ❖ ❖

Eglantine

From Latin, meaning 'small needle.'

Eléonore
From Latin, meaning 'God is my light.'
Variants: Aliénor, Aliénore, Léonor.
Famous bearer of the name: Eleanor Roosevelt,
American First Lady and social activist (1884–1962).

Elisabeth
From Hebrew, meaning 'God is my satisfaction.'
Variants: Babette, Elise, Elsa, Lise, Lisette.
Famous bearer of the name: Elisabeth Vigée-Lebrun,
French portraitist (1755–1842).

Elodie
From Greek, meaning 'eulogy.'
Variant: Alodie.

Elvire
From Saxon, meaning 'white.'
Variant: Alvira.

Emilie
From Latin, meaning 'rival.'
Variant: Emilienne.

Emma
From Hebrew, meaning 'God is with us.'
Variant: Emeline.
Famous bearer of the name: Emma Thompson,
British actress (born 1959).

Emmanuelle
From Hebrew, meaning 'God is with us.'
Famous bearer of the name: Emmanuelle Béart,
French actress (born 1965).

Ernestine
From German, meaning 'seriousness.'

Estelle
From Latin, meaning 'star.'
Variant: Ethelle.

Eugénie
From Greek, meaning 'of noble descent.'
Famous bearer of the name: Eugénie,
empress of France (1826–1920).

Eve
From Hebrew, meaning 'life' or 'living.'
Variant: Evelyne.

Fabienne
From Latin, meaning 'from the Roman clan of the Fabianus.'
Variant: Fabiola.

Faustine
From Latin, meaning 'fortunate.'

Félicie
From Latin, meaning 'happy.'
Variants: Félicienne, Félicité.

Fernande
From German, meaning 'adventurous journey.'

Flavie
From Latin, meaning 'blond
(as the members of the Roman clan of the Flavius).'

Flora

From Latin, meaning 'flower.'
Variants: Fleur, Florie, Florine.
Famous bearer of the name: Flora Tristan, feminist and
grandmother of the painter Paul Gauguin (1803–1844).

Florence

From Latin, meaning 'flourishing.'
Variants: Fleurance, Florentia, Florentine.
Famous bearer of the name: Florence Nightingale,
British nurse, hospital reformer and humanitarian (1820–1910).

Françoise

The French form of Frances. From Latin,
meaning 'from France.'
Variants: Fanny, France, Franceline, Francette, Francine.
Famous bearer of the name: Françoise Sagan,
French novelist and playwright (born 1935);
Fanny Ardant, French actress (born 1949).

Frédérique

From German, a combination of the words 'peace' and 'ruler.'

Gabrielle
From Hebrew, meaning 'power of God.'
Famous bearer of the name: Gabrielle Bonheur (pseudonym:
Coco Chanel), French fashion designer (1883–1971).

Gaëlle
From German, meaning 'stranger.'

Gaétane
From Latin, meaning 'from the Gulf and
the region of Gaéta in Italy.'

Geneviève
From German, meaning 'noble wife' or 'young lady.'
Variant: Ginette.
Famous bearer of the name: Geneviève Bujold,
French-Canadian actress (born 1942).

Georgette
From Greek, meaning 'land worker.'
Variant: Georgia, Georgina, Georgine.

Géraldine
From German, a combination of the words 'spear' and 'rule.'
Variant: Géralde.
Famous bearer of the name: Geraldine Chaplin,
American actress (born 1944).

Germaine
From Latin, meaning 'from the Germanic lands.'
Variant: Germane.
Famous bearer of the name: Germaine de Staël,
French writer and intellectual (1766–1817).

Géronima
From Greek, meaning 'sacred name.'

Gervaise
A combination of the German 'spear' and Celtic 'servant.'

Ghislaine
From German, meaning 'pledge.'

Gilberte
From German, meaning 'from high descent.'
Variant: Gisberte.

Gisèle
From German, meaning 'arrow.'
Variant: Giselle.

Grâce
From Latin, meaning 'grace.'
Variants: Gracianne, Gracieuse.

Gwendoline
From Celtic, meaning 'white circle.'

Hélène
From Greek, meaning 'bright.'
Variants: Elaine, Hélaine.
Famous bearer of the name: Hélène Madison,
American swimmer (1913–1970).

❦ ❦ ❦

Héloise
From German, a combination of 'hale' and 'wide.'

❦ ❦ ❦

Henriette
From German, meaning 'ruler of the home' or
'ruler of the house.'
Variant: Riqua.

❦ ❦ ❦

Honorine
From Latin, meaning 'honored.'

❦ ❦ ❦

Hortense
From Latin, meaning 'garden.'
Variant: Hortensia.
Famous bearer of the name: Hortense de Beauharnais,
mother of Napoleon III (1783–1837).

Huguette
From German, meaning 'intelligence.'

Hyacinthe
From Greek, derived from the flower hyacinth.
Variant: Jacinthe.

I

Inès
From Latin, meaning 'lamb.'
Variant: Inessa.

Irène
From Greek, meaning 'peace.'
Famous bearer of the name: Irène Joliot-Curie,
French physicist and Nobel laureate (1897–1956).

Isabelle
A variant of the name Elisabeth. From Hebrew,
meaning 'God is my satisfaction.'
Variants: Isabeau, Iseline.
Famous bearer of the name: Isabelle Huppert, French actress
(born 1955); Isabelle Adjani, French actress (born 1955).

J

Jacinthe
From Greek, meaning 'jacinth, a flower from
the family of hyacinths.'

Jacqueline
From Hebrew, meaning 'someone who is favored or
protected by God.'
Variants: Jacquemine, Jacquette, Jacquine, Jacquotte.
Famous bearer of the name: Jacqueline Kennedy Onassis,
American First Lady (1929–1994); Jacqueline Bisset,
British actress (born 1944)

Jeanne
From Hebrew, meaning 'God is merciful.'
Variant: Jeannine.
Famous bearer of the name: Jeanne Moreau,
French theater and motion-picture actress (born 1928).

Joëlle
From Hebrew, meaning 'Jehovah is God.'
Variants: Jodelle, Yoëlle.

Joséphine
From Hebrew, meaning 'may God add.'
Variants: Josepha, Josette, Josiane.
Famous bearer of the name: Joséphine de Beauharnais,
wife of Napoleon I (1763–1814).

Judith
From Hebrew, meaning 'jewess.'
Variant: Judie.

Julie
From Latin, meaning 'from the Roman clan of Julius Caesar.'
Variant: Julienne, Juliette.
Famous bearer of the name: Juliette Récamier,
French society leader (1777–1849); Juliette Binoche,
French actress (born 1964).

Justine
From Latin, meaning 'reasonable' or 'just.'
Variant: Juste.

L

Laetitia
From Latin, meaning 'joy.'
Alternative spelling: Létitia.
Famous bearer of the name: Laetitia Bonaparte,
mother of Napoleon I (1750–1836).

Laure
From Latin, meaning 'laurel.'
Variant: Laura.

Laurence
From Latin, meaning 'crowned with laurel.'
Variants: Laurentine, Laurette.

Léonie
From Greek, meaning 'lion.'
Variants: Léonille, Léontine.
Famous bearer of the name: Nelly Leonie Sachs,
German-Swedish poet (1891–1970).

Léopoldine
From German, meaning 'courageous nation.'

Louise
From German, meaning 'glory at war.'
Variants: Louisiane, Louisette, Lousiane.
Famous bearer of the name: Louise Florence d'Epinay,
French writer (1726–1783); Louise Erdrich,
American writer (born 1954).

Lucie
From Latin, meaning 'full of light.'
Variants: Luce, Lucette, Lucille.

Lucienne
From Latin, meaning 'luminous.'
Variant: Luciana.

Lydie
From Latin, meaning 'from the region of Lydia in Asia Minor.'
Variants: Lydia, Lydiane.

Madeleine
From Hebrew, meaning 'from Magdala in Galilea.'
Variants: Madeline, Maud.
Famous bearer of the name: Madeleine de Scudéry,
French novelist (1607–1701).

Manon
From Hebrew, meaning 'water drop.'

Marcelle
From Latin, meaning 'sacred to God Mars.'
Alternative spelling: Marcelline.

Marguerite
From Greek, meaning 'pearl.'
Variants: Margaux, Margot, Marguerie, Magali.
Famous bearer of the name: Marguerite Yourcenar,
French writer (1903–1987).

Marianne

From Hebrew, meaning 'wished-for child' and 'grace.'
Alternative spelling: Marie-Anne.
Famous bearer of the name: Marie-Anne de Cupis de Camargo,
French ballerina (1710–1770).

Marie

From Hebrew, meaning 'wished-for child.'
Variants: Marielle, Mariette, Marion.
Famous bearer of the name: Marie Curie,
French physicist (1867–1934).

Marie-Claire

From Hebrew, meaning 'wished-for child' and Latin 'clear.'
Famous bearer of the name: Marie Claire Blais,
French-Canadian writer (born 1939).

Marie-Claude

From Hebrew, meaning 'wished-for child' and Latin 'lame.'

Marie-Françoise

From Hebrew, meaning 'wished-for child' and
Latin 'from France.'
Variant: Marie-France.
Famous bearer of the name: Marie-France Pisier,
French actress (born 1944).

Marie-Josephe
From Hebrew, meaning 'wished-for child' and 'may God add.'

Marie-Louise
From Hebrew, meaning 'wished-for child' and
German 'glory at war.'
Variants: Maryse, Marie-Lou.
Famous bearer of the name: Marie-Louise de la Ramée
(pseudonym: Ouida), British novelist (1839–1908).

Marie-Madeleine
From Hebrew, meaning 'wished-for child' and
'woman from Magdala in Galilea.'
Famous bearer of the name: Marie-Madeleine Pioche de la
Vergne Comtesse de la Fayette, French novelist (1634–1693).

Marie-Thérèse
From Hebrew, meaning 'wished-for child' and
Latin 'from Therasia in the Aegean Sea.'

Marthe
From Aramaic, meaning 'lady.'

Martine
From Latin, meaning 'warrior.'

Mathilde

From German, a combination of 'strength' and 'battle.'
Variant: Mathilda.
Famous bearer of the name: Mathilda May,
French actress (born 1965).

❦ ❦ ❦

Maximilienne

From Latin, meaning 'the biggest.'

❦ ❦ ❦

Mélanie

From Greek, meaning 'black.'
Variants: Mélina, Mélinda.
Famous bearer of the name: Mélanie Klein,
Austrian psychoanalyst (1882–1960).

❦ ❦ ❦

Michèle

From Hebrew, meaning 'who is like God.'
Alternative spelling: Michelle.
Variant: Micheline.
Famous bearer of the name: Michèle Morgan,
French actress (born 1920); Michelle Pfeiffer,
American motion-picture actress (born 1957).

❦ ❦ ❦

Mireille

From Latin, meaning 'look closely.'
Variants: Mirella, Miriella.

Monique
From Greek, meaning 'alone.'

Muriel
From Gaelic, a combination of 'sea' and 'bright.'
Variant: Murielle.

Nadine
The French form of the Russian name Nadja, meaning 'hope.'
Famous bearer of the name: Nadine Gordimer,
South-African writer and Nobel laureate (born 1923).

Nathalie
From Latin, meaning 'birthday.'
Famous bearer of the name: Nathalie Sarraute, Russian-born
French novelist and playwright (born 1902).

Nicole
From Greek, meaning 'victory of the people.'
Variant: Colette, Nicolette.

Noëlle
From Hebrew, meaning 'birthday.'
Variant: Noëllie, Noelie.

Odette
From German, meaning 'wealth.'
Variants: Odile.

𝔓

Pascale
From Greek, meaning 'of Easter.'
Variant: Pascaline.

Patricia
From Latin, meaning 'noble, from the Roman aristocracy.'

Paulette
From Latin, meaning 'small.'
Variant: Pauline.
Famous bearer of the name: Paulette Goddard,
Amerian actress (1911–1990).

Pétronille
From Latin, meaning 'from the Roman clan of the Petronius.'

Philippine
From Greek, meaning 'who loves horses.'

Pierrette
From Greek, meaning 'stone.'

Régine
From Latin, meaning 'queen.'
Variant: Réjane.

❖ ❖ ❖

Reine
From French, meaning 'queen.'

❖ ❖ ❖

Renée
From Latin, meaning 'reborn.'

❖ ❖ ❖

Romane
From Latin, meaning 'from Rome.'
Variant: Romana.

❖ ❖ ❖

Rosalie
From Latin, meaning 'rose and lily.'
Variants: Rosaline, Roseline.
Famous bearer of the name: Rosaline Bernard (pseudonym:
Sarah Bernhardt), French actress (1844–1923).

 ❖ ❖ ❖

Rose
From Latin, meaning 'rose.'
Variants: Rosée, Rosette.

Sabine
From Latin, meaning 'from the tribe of the Sabines
in ancient Rome.'
Variants: Sabrina, Savine.

Sandrine
A variant of Alexandra, From Greek,
meaning 'defender of men.'
Variant: Sandra.
Famous bearer of the name: Sandrine Bonnaire,
French actress (born 1967).

Sébastienne
From Greek, meaning 'adored.'
Variant: Bastienne.

Ségolène
From German, meaning 'victory.'
Variant: Sigolène.

Séraphine
From Hebrew, meaning 'fiery.'
Variant: Séraphina.

Sergine
From Latin, probably derived from a Roman clan name.

Séverine
From Latin, meaning 'vigorous.'

Sibylle
From Greek, meaning 'prophetess who knows the divine will.'
Variants: Sibille, Sybille.

Sidonie
From Latin, meaning 'from the Phoenician town of Sidon.'
Famous bearer of the name: Sidonie Gabrielle Claudine Colette,
French novelist (1873–1954).

Simone
From Hebrew, meaning 'listening.'
Variant: Simonette.
Famous bearer of the name: Simone de Beauvoir, French writer
(1908–1986); Simone Signoret, French actress (1921–1985).

Solange
From Latin, meaning 'solemn.'
Variant: Solène, Solenne.

Sophie
From Greek, meaning 'wisdom.'
Famous bearer of the name: Sophie Marceau,
French actress (born 1966).

Stéphane
From Greek, meaning 'crown of glory.'
Variant: Stéphanie.
Famous bearer of the name: Stéphane Audran,
French actress (born 1939).

Suzanne
From Hebrew, meaning 'lily.'
Variants: Suzette, Suzon.
Famous bearer of the name: Suzanne Valadon, painter and
mother of the painter Maurice Utrillo (1867–1955);
Suzanne Farrell, American ballet dancer (born 1945).

Sylvie
From Latin, meaning 'from the forest.'
Variants: Sylvaine, Sylvette, Sylviane.

T

Thérèse
From Latin, meaning 'from Therasia in the Aegean Sea.'
Variant: Térésa.

Théodora
From Greek, meaning 'gift from God.'
Variants: Dora, Dorine.
Famous bearer of the name: Dora Maar (born Théodora Markovitch), photographer and painter and companion of Pablo Picasso (1907–1997).

ℭ

Ursule
From Latin, meaning 'bear.'
Variants: Ursula, Ursuline.
Famous bearer of the name: Ursula K. LeGuin,
American fantasy and science-fiction writer (born 1929).

Valentine
From Latin, meaning 'strong.'
Variant: Valentina.

Valérie
From Latin, meaning 'valorous.'
Variant: Valérianne.

Véronique
From Latin, meaning 'true picture.'

Victoire
From French, meaning 'victory.'
Variant: Victorine.

❖ ❖ ❖

Violette
From Latin, meaning 'violet.'
Variants: Violaine.

Virginie
From Latin, meaning 'virgin.'

Viviane
From Latin, meaning 'alive.'
Variant: Vivence.

Xavière
From Basque, meaning 'new home.'
Variant: Xaveria.

Yolande
From Latin, meaning 'violet.'
Variant: Yolaine.

Yvette
From Celtic, meaning 'yew.'
Variants: Ivette, Yveline, Yvonne.

Z

Zoé
From Greek, meaning 'life.'

Boys' Names

Abélard
From Hebrew, meaning 'breath.'

Adelphe
From German, a combination of the words 'noble' and 'wolf.'

Adrien
From Latin, meaning 'from the Adria' or 'from the Adriatic sea.'
Alternative spelling: Hadrien.
Famous bearer of the name: Claude Adrien Helvétius,
French philosopher (1715–1771).

Aimable
French, meaning 'lovable.'

Aimé
French, meaning 'loved.'
Famous bearer of the name: Aimé Césaire,
poet from Martinique (born 1913).

Alain
The French form of Alan. From Celtic, meaning 'harmony.'
Variant: Alois.
Famous bearers of the name: Alain Resnais, French film
director (born 1922); Alain Delon, French actor (born 1935).

Alban
From Latin, meaning 'from the town of Alba.'
Famous bearer of the name: Alban Berg,
Austrian composer (1885–1935).

❖ ❖ ❖

Albéric
From German, meaning 'Lord of the Elves.'

Albert
From German, meaning 'illustrious.'
Variants: Adalbert, Aubert.
Famous bearers of the name: Albert Camus, French-Algerian
writer (1913–1960); Philippe Joseph Aubert de Gaspé,
French-Canadian novelist (1786–1871).

Albin
From Latin, meaning 'white.'
Variant: Aubin.
Famous bearer of the name: Albin Michel,
French publisher (1873–1943).

Alèthe
From Greek, meaning 'truth.'

Alexandre
From Greek, meaning 'defender of men.'
Famous bearer of the name: Alexandre Dumas père,
French writer (1802–1870).

Alexis
From Greek, meaning 'defender' or 'helper.'
Famous bearer of the name: Alexis Carrel, French surgeon and
Nobel laureate (1873–1944).

Alfred
From Old English, meaning 'old peace.'
Famous bearers of the name: Alfred, Lord Tennyson,
English poet (1809–1892); Alfred de Musset,
French writer (1810–1857).

Alois

The Provençal form of Louis.
Alternative spelling: Aloys.

Alphonse

From German, meaning 'ready to fight.'
Famous bearers of the name: Alphonse de Lamartine,
French poet (1790–1869); Alphonse Daudet,
French writer (1840–1897).

Amand

From Latin, meaning 'lovable.'

Ambroise

From Greek, meaning 'immortal.'
Famous bearer of the name: Ambroise Paré,
French surgeon (c. 1509–1590).

Amédée

From Latin, meaning 'who loves God.'
Famous bearer of the name: Jules Amédée Barbey d'Aurevilly,
French novelist and critic (1808–1889).

Anastase

From Greek, meaning 'resurrection.'

Anatole

From Greek, meaning 'dawn.'
Famous bearer of the name: Anatole France,
French writer (1844–1924).

André

The French form of Andrew. From Greek, meaning
'male' or 'manly.'
Variants: Andrieu, Andor.
Famous bearer of the name: André Malraux,
French writer (1901–1976).

Anselme

From German, a combination of 'God' and 'helmet.'
Variant: Anthelme.

Antoine

The French form of Anthony. From Latin, meaning 'from the
Roman clan of the Antonius.'
Variants: Antoinet, Antonin.
Famous bearers of the name: Antoine de St-Exupéry,
French writer (1900–1944); Antonin Artaud, French poet,
dramatist, and actor (1896–1948).

Apollinaire
From Greek, meaning 'of Apollo, the Greek and Roman God of sunlight, prophecy, music, and poetry.'

Arcadius
From Greek, meaning 'from Arcadia.'
Variant: Arcady.

Archibald
From German, a combination of 'true' and 'bold.'
Famous bearer of the name: Archibald MacLeish,
American poet, social critic and educator (1892–1982).

Aristide
From Greek, meaning 'son of the best.'
Famous bearer of the name: Aristide Briand,
French statesman (1862–1932).

Armand
The French form of Herman. From German, meaning
'strong man.'
Variant: Armandin.
Famous bearer of the name: Armand Peugeot,
French car maker (1849–1915).

Arnaud

The French form of Arnold. From German, meaning
'strong eagle.'
Alternative spellings: Arnaut, Arnault.

Arsène

From Greek, meaning 'virile' or 'strong.'

Arthur

From Celtic, meaning 'bear.'
Variant: Artus.
Famous bearer of the name: Arthur Rimbaud,
French poet (1854–1891).

Athanase

From Greek, meaning 'immortal.'

Auguste

From Latin, meaning 'venerable.'
Variant: Augustin.
Famous bearers of the name: Auguste Rodin, French sculptor
(1840–1917); Auguste Renoir, French painter (1841–1919).

Aurèle
From Latin, meaning 'from the Roman clan of the Aurelius.'
Variant: Aurélien.

❧ ❧ ❧

Aymeric
From German, meaning 'lively as a falcon.'

ℬ

Baptiste
From Greek, meaning 'baptized.'

Barnabé
From Hebrew, meaning 'son of consolation.'

Barthélémy
The French form of Bartholomew. From Hebrew, meaning 'son of Talmai.'
Variant: Bartolomé.

Basile
From Greek, meaning 'king.'
Variant: Basilide.

Baudouin
The French form of Baldwin. From German, meaning 'bold friend.'
Alternative spelling: Beaudoin.
Famous bearer of the name: Baudouin,
king of Belgium (1930–1993).

Benjamin

From Hebrew, meaning 'preferred son.'
Famous bearer of the name: Benjamin Constant,
French politician and writer (1767–1830).

Benoît

From Latin, meaning 'protected by God' or 'blessed.'
Famous bearer of the name: Benoît B. Mandelbrot,
Polish-born French mathematician (born 1924).

Bérenger

From German, a combination of the words 'bear' and 'spear.'
Alternative spelling: Béranger.

Bernard

From German, meaning 'courageous bear.'
Variants: Barnard, Bernardin.
Famous bearer of the name: Bernard Hinault,
French cyclist (born 1954).

Bertrand

From German, meaning 'magnificent crow.'
Famous bearers of the name: Bertrand Russell,
British philosopher, mathematician and Nobel laureate
(1872–1970); Bertrand Tavernier, French motion-picture
director and screenwriter (born 1941).

Blaise
From Latin, meaning 'stammering.'
Famous bearer of the name: Blaise Pascal, French philosopher
and mathematician (1623–1662).

Boniface
From Latin, meaning 'well-doer.'

❧ ❧ ❧

Brice
From Celtic, meaning 'sublime.'
Variant: Brix.
Famous bearer of the name: Brice Marden, American painter,
draftsman, and printmaker (born 1938).

❧ ❧ ❧

Bruno
From German, meaning 'brown.'
Famous bearer of the name: Bruno Walter,
German-born American conductor (1876–1962).

ℭ

Camille

From Latin, name borne by servants of certain priests in
ancient Rome.
Famous bearer of the name: Camille Pisarro,
French painter (1830–1903).

Candide

From Latin, meaning 'shining white.'

Cédric

From Celtic, meaning 'first choice.'
Variant: Cédar.

Célestin

From Latin, meaning 'heavenly.'

Césaire

From Latin, meaning 'from the Roman clan of
Gaius Julius Caesar.'
Variant: César.

Charles
From German, meaning 'courageous bear.'
Variant: Charlot.
Famous bearer of the name: Charles de Gaulle,
French statesman (1890–1970); Charles Aznavour,
French singer and actor (born 1924).

Christian
From Greek, meaning 'disciple of Christ.'
Variant: Chrétien.
Famous bearers of the name: Chrétien de Troyes,
French poet (1160–1190); Christian Dior,
French fashion designer (1905–1957).

Christophe
The French form of Christopher. From Greek, meaning
'someone who carries the Christ in his heart.'

Claude
From Latin, meaning 'lame.'
Variant: Claudien.
Famous bearer of the name: Claude Monet,
French painter (1840–1926); Claude Berri,
French movie director (born 1934).

Clément
From Latin, meaning 'mild' or 'merciful.'
Famous bearer of the name: Clément Marot,
French poet (1496–1544).

Colomban
From Latin, derived from 'dove.'

Constantin
The French form of Constantine. From Latin, meaning
'constant.'
Variant: Constant.
Famous bearer of the name: Constantin Brancusi,
Romanian-born French sculptor (1876–1957).

Corentin
From Celtic, probably derived from 'raven.'

Cyprien
From Latin, meaning 'from Cyprus.'

Cyrille
The French form of Cyril. From Greek, meaning 'lord'

Damien
From Greek, meaning 'sacred to Damia,
the Goddess of growth.'
Famous bearer of the name: Father Damien
(Joseph Damine de Veuster), Belgian Roman Catholic
missionary to the lepers of Hawaii (1840–1889).

Daniel
From Hebrew, meaning 'God is the (only) judge.'
Famous bearer of the name: Daniel Bernoulli,
Dutch-born Swiss scientist (1700–1782); Daniel Auteuil,
French actor (born 1950).

David
From Hebrew, meaning 'beloved.'
Famous bearer of the name: David D'Angers,
French sculptor (1788–1856).

Denis
From Greek, meaning 'sacred to Dionysus, the God of wine and fertile crops.'
Alternative spelling: Denys.
Variant: Dion.
Famous bearer of the name: Denis Diderot,
French encyclopedist and philosopher (1713–1784).

❦ ❦ ❦

Désiré
French, meaning 'desired.'

❦ ❦ ❦

Didier
From Latin, meaning 'desired.'

❦ ❦ ❦

Dieudonné
French, meaning 'given by God.'

❦ ❦ ❦

Dominique
The French form of Dominic. From Latin, meaning
'someone who belongs to God.'
Variant: Domien.
Famous bearer of the name: Dominique François Jean Arago,
French astronomer and physicist (1786–1853).

❦ ❦ ❦

Donatien
From Latin, meaning 'given.'

Edgar
From German, meaning 'defender of the good.'
Famous bearer of the name: Edgar Degas,
French painter (1834–1917).

Edmond
From Old English, a combination of 'rich' and 'protection.'
Famous bearer of the name: Edmond Rostand,
French author of romantic plays (1868–1918).

Edouard
The French form of Edward. From Old English,
a combination of 'rich' and 'guardian.'
Famous bearer of the name: Edouard Manet,
French painter (1832–1883).

Emeric
From German, meaning 'vivid as a falcon.'

Emile
From Latin, meaning 'rival.'
Variant: Emilien.
Famous bearer of the name: Emile Zola,
French writer (1840–1902).

Eric
From German, meaning 'rich in honors.'
Alternative spelling: Erik.
Famous bearer of the name: Erik Satie,
French composer (1866–1925); Eric Rohmer,
French movie director (born 1920).

Ernest
From German, meaning 'seriousness.'
Famous bearer of the name: Ernest Bloch,
Swiss-American composer (1880–1959).

Etienne
From Greek, meaning 'crown of glory.'
Variant: Stéphane.
Famous bearer of the name: Etienne Brûlé,
French explorer (c. 1592–1632).

Eugène
From Greek, meaning 'of noble descent.'
Variant: Eugénien.
Famous bearer of the name: Eugène Delacroix,
French painter (1798–1863).

Eustache
From Greek, meaning 'fruitful.'
Famous bearer of the name: Eustache Deschamps,
French poet (c. 1340–1407).

Evrard
From German, a combination of the words 'boar' and 'hard.'

Fabien

From Latin, meaning 'from the Roman clan of the Fabianus.'
Famous bearer of the name: Pär Fabien Lagerkvist,
Swedish writer and Nobel laureate (1891–1974).

Fabrice

From Latin, meaning 'blacksmith.'
Variant: Fabricien.

Faustin

From Latin, meaning 'fortunate.'

Félicien

From Latin, meaning 'happy.'
Variant: Félix.
Famous bearer of the name: Félix Bloch,
Swiss-born American physicist (1905–1983).

Ferdinand

From German, meaning 'venturous journey.'
Variant: Fernand.
Famous bearers of the name: Ferdinand Brunétière,
French literary critic (1849–1906); Fernand Léger,
French painter (1881–1955).

Fidèle

French, meaning 'faithful' or 'loyal.'

Firmin

From Latin, meaning 'steadfast' or 'constant.'

Flavien

From Latin, meaning 'blond
(as the members of the Roman clan of the Flavius).'

Florent

From Latin, meaning 'flourishing.'
Variant: Florentin.
Famous bearer of the name: Florent Carton d' Ancourt,
French comic playwright (1661–1725).

François
The French form of Francis. From Latin, meaning
'from France.'
Variants: Francis, Francelin.
Famous bearers of the name: François Rabelais,
French writer (c. 1494–1553); François Truffaut,
French film director (1932–1984).

Frédéric
The French form of Frederick. From German,
a combination of the words 'peace' and 'ruler.'
Alternative spelling: Frédérick.
Famous bearer of the name: Frédéric Chopin,
Polish composer and pianist (1810–1840).

Fulbert
From German, meaning 'very bright.'

Gabriel
From Hebrew, meaning 'power of God.'
Famous bearer of the name: Gabriel Marcel,
French philosopher (1889–1973).

Gaël
From German, meaning 'stranger.'

❖ ❖ ❖

Gaétan
From Latin, meaning 'from the Gulf and the region of
Gaeta in Italy.'
Famous bearer of the name: Gaétan Vestris,
French ballet dancer (1729–1808).

❖ ❖ ❖

Gaspard
The French form of Jasper. From Persian, meaning
'keeper of treasure.'
Variants: Caspar, Gasparin.
Famous bearer of the name: Gaspard Monge,
French mathematician and inventor of
descriptive geometry (1746–1818).

Gaston

From German, meaning 'traveler' or 'host.'
Famous bearer of the name: Gaston Lachaise,
French-American sculptor (1882–1935).

Gautier

From German, meaning 'army.'
Alternative spelling: Gaultier.
Famous bearer of the name: Gautier de Lille,
poet (13TH century).

Geoffroy

From German, meaning 'peace of God.'
Alternative spelling: Geoffroi.
Famous bearer of the name: Geoffroy de Beaulieu,
friend of Louis IX (13TH century).

Georges

From Greek, meaning 'land worker.'
Famous bearer of the name: Georges Braque,
French painter (1882–1963).

Gérald

From German, a combination of the words 'spear' and 'rule.'
Variants: Géraud, Giraud.

Gérard

From German, meaning 'hard, bold spear.'
Variant: Girard.
Famous bearer of the name: Gérard Philipe,
French actor (1922–1959); Gérard Depardieu,
French actor (born 1948).

❖ ❖ ❖

Germain

From Latin, meaning 'from the Germanic lands.'
Variants: German, Garmon.
Famous bearer of the name: Germain Pilon,
French sculptor (c. 1530–1590).

❖ ❖ ❖

Gervais

A combination of the German 'spear' and Celtic 'servant.'

❖ ❖ ❖

Ghislain

From German, meaning 'pledge.'

❖ ❖ ❖

Gilbert

From German, meaning 'from high descent.'
Famous bearer of the name: Gilbert Parker,
Canadian novelist and poet (1862–1932).

Gilles

The French form of Giles. Probably from Latin, meaning 'jester.'
Variant: Gil.
Famous bearer of the name: Pierre-Gilles de Gennes,
French physicist and Nobel laureate (born 1932).

Godefroy

The French form of Godfrey. From German, meaning
'peace of God.'
Alternative spelling: Godfrey.
Famous bearer of the name: Godfrey of Bouillon,
French nobleman and leader of the first crusade (c. 1061–1100).

Gonzague

Derived from the name of a royal Italian family.

Grégoire

The French form of Gregory. From Greek, meaning
'who watches.'
Variants: Grégori, Grégory.

Guillaume

The French form of William. From German, meaning 'will.'
Famous bearer of the name: Guillaume Apollinaire,
French poet (1880–1918).

Gustave
From German, meaning 'prosperous.'
Famous bearer of the name: Gustave Flaubert,
French novelist (1821–1880).

Guy
From German, meaning 'forest.'
Variant: Guyot.
Famous bearer of the name: Guy de Maupassant,
French writer (1850–1893).

Gwénaël
From Celtic, meaning 'white' or 'fair.'

Hector
From Greek, meaning 'holding fast.'
Famous bearer of the name: Hector Berlioz,
French composer (1803–1869).

Henri
From German, meaning 'ruler of the home' or
'ruler of the house.'
Famous bearers of the name: Henri Rousseu
(called le Douanier), self-taught French artist (1844–1910);
Henri de Toulouse-Lautrec, French painter (1864–1901);
Henri Matisse, French artist (1869–1954).

Hermès
From Hermes, the Greek God of commerce, eloquence,
invention, travel and theft.

❀ ❀ ❀

Hervé
From Celtic, meaning 'strong.'
Variant: Herviel.

Hilaire
From Latin, meaning 'cheerful.'

Hippolyte
From Greek, a combination of the words 'horse' and 'let loose.'
Famous bearer of the name: Jean Hippolyte Giraudoux,
French writer (1882–1944).

Honoré
From Latin, meaning 'honored.'
Famous bearer of the name: Honoré de Balzac,
French novelist (1799–1850).

Hubert
From German, meaning 'brilliant.'
Variant: Huibert.

Hugues
The French form of Hugh. From German, meaning
'intelligence.'
Variants: Hugo, Hugolin.

J

Ignace
From Latin, meaning 'fiery.'

Isidore
From Greek, meaning 'gift of Isis.'
Famous bearer of the name: Maximilien François Marie Isidore de Robespierre, French lawyer and politician (1758–1794).

J

Jacques
The French form of Jack. From Hebrew, meaning
'someone who is favored or protected by God.'
Variant: Jacquot.
Famous bearer of the name: Jacques Derrida,
French philosopher (born 1930); Jacques-Yves Cousteau,
French marine explorer, author and filmmaker (1910–1997).

Jean
The French form of John. From Hebrew, 'God is merciful.'
Famous bearer of the name: Jean Anouilh,
French playwright (1910–1987).

Jean-Baptiste
From Hebrew 'God is merciful' and Greek-Latin
'someone who baptizes.'
Famous bearer of the name: Jean-Baptiste Poquelin (Molière),
French dramatist, comedy writer and actor (1622–1673).

Jean-Bernard
From Hebrew 'God is merciful' and German 'courageous bear.'
Famous bearer of the name: Jean-Bernard Léon Foucault,
French physicist (1819–1868).

Jean-Charles
From Hebrew 'God is merciful' and German 'courageous bear.'

Jean-Claude
From Hebrew 'God is merciful' and Latin 'lame.'
Famous bearer of the name: Jean-Claude Killy,
French skiing champion (born 1943).

Jean-Emile
From Hebrew 'God is merciful' and Latin 'rival.'

Jean-François
From Hebrew 'God is merciful' and Latin 'from France.'
Famous bearer of the name: Jean-François Champollion,
French Egyptologist (1790–1832).

Jean-Jacques
From Hebrew 'God is merciful' and 'someone who is
favored or protected by God.'
Famous bearer of the name: Jean-Jacques Rousseau,
French philosopher (1712–1778); Jean-Jacques Annaud,
French movie director (born 1943).

Jean-Joseph
From Hebrew 'God is merciful' and 'may God add.'
Famous bearer of the name: Urbain Jean-Joseph Leverrier,
French astronomer (1811–1877).

Jean-Louis
From Hebrew 'God is merciful' and German 'glory at war.'
Famous bearer of the name: Jean-Louis Barrault,
French actor and director (1910–1994); Jean-Louis Trintignant,
French actor (born 1930).

Jean-Luc
From Hebrew 'God is merciful' and Latin 'light.'
Famous bearer of the name: Jean-Luc Godard,
French motion-picture director (born 1930).

Jean-Marc
From Hebrew 'God is merciful' and Latin
'sacred to the god Mars.'
Famous bearer of the name: Jean-Marc Nattier,
French miniature painter (1685–1766).

Jean-Marie
From Hebrew 'God is merciful' and the French form of Mary.
Famous bearer of the name: Jean-Marie Comte de Villiers de
l'Isle-Adam, French writer (1838–1889).

Jean-Michel
From Hebrew 'God is merciful' and 'like God.'
Famous bearer of the name: Jean-Michel Basquiat,
American painter (1960–1988).

Jean-Paul
From Hebrew 'God is merciful' and Latin 'small.'
Famous bearer of the name: Jean-Paul Belmondo,
French actor (born 1930).

Jean-Pierre
From Hebrew 'God is merciful' and Latin 'stone.'
Famous bearer of the name: Jean-Pierre Rampal,
flutist (born 1922).

Jérémie
From Hebrew, meaning 'may God exalt.'

Jérôme
From Greek, meaning 'sacred name.'
Famous bearer of the name: Jérôme Bonaparte,
youngest brother of Napoleon (1784–1860).

Joël
From Hebrew, meaning 'Jehovah is God.'

Joseph
From Hebrew, meaning 'may God add.'
Variant: José.
Famous bearer of the name: Joseph Kessel,
French writer (1898–1979).

Jules
The French form of Julius. From Latin, meaning
'from the Roman clan of Julius Caesar.'
Variant: Julien.
Famous bearer of the name: Jules Vernes,
French science-fiction writer (1828–1905).

Justin
From Latin, meaning 'reasonable' or 'just.'
Variant: Juste.

Juvénal
From Latin, meaning 'youthful.'

Lambert
From German, meaning 'great country.'

Laurent
The French form of Lawrence. From Latin, meaning
'crowned with laurel.'

❖ ❖ ❖

Lazare
From Hebrew, meaning 'God is my help.'

Léon
From Latin, meaning 'lion.'
Variants: Léo, Léontin.
Famous bearer of the name: Léon Blum,
French politician (1872–1950).

Léonard
From Latin and German, meaning 'strong lion.'
Variants: Léo, Léon, Léonce.

Léopold

From German, meaning 'courageous nation.'
Famous bearer of the name: Léopold Sédar Senghar,
first president of Senegal (born 1906).

Lionel

From Latin, meaning 'small lion.'
Variant: Lyonel.
Famous bearer of the name: Lyonel Feininger,
American painter (1871–1956).

Louis

From German, meaning 'glory at war.'
Variant: Lou.
Famous bearer of the name: Louis Aragon,
French writer (1897–1982); Louis Malle,
French film director (born 1932).

Lucas

The French form of Luke. From Latin, meaning 'light.'
Variant: Luc.
Famous bearer of the name: Luc Besson,
French movie director (born 1959).

Lucien

From Latin, meaning 'full of light.'
Famous bearer of the name: Lucien Bonaparte,
brother of Napoleon (1775–1840).

Ludovic

From German, meaning 'glory at the fight.'
Famous bearer of the name: Ludovic Halévy,
French writer (1834–1908).

ℳ

Maël
From Celtic, meaning 'devotee.'

Marc
From Latin, meaning 'sacred to the god Mars.'
Variants: Marceau, Marcien.
Famous bearer of the name: Marc Chagall,
Russian-born French painter (1887–1985).

Marcel
The French form of Marcellus. From Latin, meaning
'sacred to the god Mars.'
Variant: Marcellin.
Famous bearer of the name: Marcel Proust,
French writer (1871–1922); Marcel Pagnol,
French movie director (1985–1974).

Marin
From Latin, meaning 'man of the sea.'

Marius
From Latin, meaning 'from the Roman clan of the Marius.'

Martin

From Latin, meaning 'warrior.'
Variants: Martien, Martinien.
Famous bearer of the name: Martin Fréminet,
French painter (1567–1619).

Matthieu

The French form of Matthew. From Hebrew 'given by God,'
Alternative spelling: Mathieu.
Famous bearer of the name: Mathieu Le Nain,
French painter (1607–1677).

Maurice

The French form of Morris. From Latin, meaning
'Moorish' or 'African.'
Famous bearer of the name: Maurice Ravel,
French composer (1875–1937); Maurice Chevalier,
French actor (1888–1972).

Maxime

From Latin, meaning 'the biggest.'
Variants: Maximin, Maximilien.
Famous bearer of the name: Maxime Duchamp,
French painter of the Dada movement (1887–1968).

Médard
From German, meaning 'strong.'

❖ ❖ ❖

Melaine
From Greek, meaning 'brown' or 'dark.'

❖ ❖ ❖

Michel
The French form of Michael. From Hebrew, meaning
'who is like God.'
Variant: Michou.
Famous bearers of the name: Michel de Montaigne,
French writer (1533–1592); Michel Foucault,
French philosopher (1926–1984); Michel Piccoli,
French actor (born 1925).

❖ ❖ ❖

Modeste
French, meaning 'modest.'
Famous bearer of the name: André Ernest Modeste Grétry,
Belgian composer (1741–1813).

Nicolas
The French form of Nicholas. From Greek, meaning
'victory of the people.'
Variant: Nicolin.
Famous bearer of the name: Nicolas Poussin,
French painter (1594–1665).

Noé
The French form of Noah. From Hebrew, meaning 'repose.'

Noël
From Latin, meaning 'birthday.'

Octave
From Latin, meaning 'eight.'
Variant: Octavien.
Famous bearer of the name: Octave Crémazie,
French-Canadian poet (1827–1879).

Olivier
The French form of Oliver. From Latin, meaning 'olive tree.'
Variant: Olier.
Famous bearer of the name: Olivier Messiaen,
French composer and organist (1908–1992).

Pacôme
From Greek, meaning 'of strong nature.'

❖ ❖ ❖

Pascal
From Greek, meaning 'of Easter.'

❖ ❖ ❖

Patrice
The French form of Patrick. From Latin, meaning 'noble, from the Roman aristocracy.'
Famous bearer of the name: Patrice Lumumba,
first Prime minister of the Republic of Congo (1925–1961);
Patrice Leconte, French movie director (born 1947).

❖ ❖ ❖

Paul
From Latin, meaning 'small.'
Variant: Paulin.
Famous bearer of the name: Paul Gauguin,
French painter (1848–1903).

❖ ❖ ❖

Philémon
From Greek, meaning 'kiss.'

Philibert

From German, meaning 'very bright.'

Philippe

From Greek, meaning 'who loves horses.'
Famous bearer of the name: Philippe de Champaigne,
French painter (1602–1674); Philippe Noiret,
French actor (born 1930).

Pierre

The French form of Peter. From Greek, meaning 'stone.'
Variants: Pierrot, Pierrick.
Famous bearer of the name: Pierre de Ronsard,
French poet (1524–1585); Pierre Arditi,
French actor (born 1944).

Placide

From Latin, meaning 'gentle' or 'peaceful.'

Pons

From Latin, meaning 'bridge.'
Variant: Pontien.

Prosper

From Latin, meaning 'prosperous.'
Variant: Prospero.
Famous bearer of the name: Prosper Mérimée,
French novelist and historian (1803–1870).

ℚ

Quentin

From Latin, meaning 'fifth.'
Alternative spelling: Quintin.
Famous bearer of the name: Quentin Massys,
Flemish painter (c. 1466–1530).

Rainier
From German, a combination of 'counsel' and 'army.'
Famous bearer of the name: Rainier III,
prince of Monaco (born 1923).

Raoul
The French form of Ralph. From Old English, a combination of
the words 'counsel' and 'wolf.'
Alternative spelling: Raul.
Variant: Roux.
Famous bearer of the name: Raoul Dufy,
French painter (1877–1965).

Raymond
From German, a combination of the words 'counsel' or 'might'
and 'protection.'
Alternative spelling: Raimond.
Famous bearer of the name: Raymond Queneau,
French novelist, poet and critic (1903–1976).

❖ ❖ ❖

Régis
From Latin, meaning 'king.'

Rémi
From Latin, meaning 'from Reims.'
Alternative spelling: Rémy.
Famous bearer of the name: Rémy de Gourmont,
French critic and writer (1858–1915).

Renaud
From German, meaning 'who governs with counsel.'
Variant: Rénald.

René
From Latin, meaning 'reborn.'
Famous bearer of the name: René Descartes,
French philosopher (1596–1650).

Richard
From German, meaning 'strong.'
Variant: Rico.

Robert
From German, meaning 'glorious' or 'brilliant.'
Variant: Robin.
Famous bearers of the name: Robert Schuman,
Luxembourg-born French statesman (1886–1953);
Robert Bresson, French film director
and scriptwriter (born 1907).

Rodolphe

The French form of Rudolph. From German, meaning 'wolf.'
Famous bearer of the name: Louis Rodolphe Agassiz,
Swiss-American naturalist (1807–1873).

Roger

From German, meaning 'sword of glory.'
Variant: Rogier.
Famous bearer of the name: Roger Martin du Gard,
French novelist, playwright and Nobel laureate (1881–1958).

Roland

From German, a combination of the words 'fame' and 'land.'
Famous bearer of the name: Roland Barthes,
French social and literary critic (1915–1980).

Romain

From Latin, meaning 'from Rome.'
Variant: Roman.
Famous bearer of the name: Romain Gary,
French writer (1914–1980).

Rufin

From Latin, meaning 'with red hair.'

Sacha
A diminutive of the Greek name Alexandre, meaning
'defender of men.'
Famous bearer of the name: Sacha Guitry,
French actor and movie director (1885–1957).

Sébastien
From Greek, meaning 'adored.'
Variants: Bastien, Bastin.

Séraphin
From Hebrew, meaning 'fiery.'

Serge
From Latin, probably derived from a Roman clan name.
Famous bearer of the name: Serge Lifar,
Russian-French dancer (1905–1986); Serge Gainsbourg,
French actor and movie director (1928–1991).

Séverin
From Latin, meaning 'rigorous.'

Simon

From Hebrew, meaning 'listening.'
Variant: Siméon.
Famous bearers of the name: Simon Vouet,
French painter (1590–1649); Jean Baptiste Siméon Chardin,
French painter (1699–1779).

❖ ❖ ❖

Stéphane

The French form of Steven. From Greek, meaning
'crown of glory.'
Variant: Etienne.
Famous bearer of the name: Stéphane Mallarmé,
French poet (1842–1898).

❖ ❖ ❖

Sylvain

From Latin, name of the god of trees and forests.
Variants: Silvan, Sylvestre.

❖ ❖ ❖

Sylvestre

From Latin, meaning 'from the woods.'

Tanguy
From Celtic, a combination of 'peace' and 'pure.'

Théodore
From Greek, meaning 'gift from God.'
Famous bearer of the name: Théodore Rousseau,
French painter (1812–1867).

Théodule
From Greek, meaning 'servant of God.'

Théophile
From Greek, meaning 'who loves God.'
Variant: Théo.
Famous bearer of the name: Théophile Gautier,
French poet, critic and novelist (1811–1872).

❖ ❖ ❖

Thibaud
From German, meaning 'audacious people.'
Alternative spellings: Thibault, Thiébault.

Thierry

From German, meaning 'powerful nation.'
Variant: Terri.
Famous bearer of the name: Thierry Lhermitte,
French actor (born 1952).

Thomas

From Aramaic, meaning 'twin.'

Toussaint

From Latin, meaning 'all saints.'

Tristan

From the Celtic name Drystan, probably meaning
'son of the wise.'
Famous bearer of the name: Tristan Tzara,
Romanian-born French essayist and poet (1896–1963).

U

Urbain
From Latin, meaning 'from the city.'
Famous bearer of the name: Urbain Leverrier,
French astronomer (1811–1877).

Valentin
From Latin, meaning 'strong.'
Variant: Valens.

Valéry
From Latin, meaning 'valorous.'
Famous bearer of the name: Valéry Giscard d'Estaing,
French statesman (born 1926).

Victor
From Latin, meaning 'victorious.'
Variants: Victorien, Victorin.
Famous bearers of the name: Victor Hugo,
French poet, novelist and playwright (1802–1885);
Victorien Sardou, French dramatist (1831–1908).

Vincent
From Latin, meaning 'to win.'
Famous bearer of the name: Stephen Vincent Benét,
American poet and novelist (1898–1943).

Xavier
From Navarre, meaning 'new house.'
Famous bearer of the name: Xavier Leroux,
composer (1863–1919).

Yann
From Brittany, variant of the name Jean, meaning
'God is merciful.'
Variant: Yannick.

Yves
From Celtic, meaning 'yew.'
Variant: Yven, Yvon.
Famous bearer of the name: Yves Montand,
French actor (1921–1996).

Z

Zéphirin
From Greek, meaning 'soft, light wind.'
Alternative spelling: Zéphyrin.

French Interest Titles from Hippocrene

French Language Guides

MASTERING FRENCH, book and audio cassettes

Twenty lessons introduce the student to basic skills for those who intend to spend some time in France or to do business with French companies. The course also provides the essentials of grammar and structures of the language, necessary for developing reading and writing skills. Each chapter has a theme or aim, a topic and related grammar. Each chapter begins with a series of dialogues, which introduce the new topics, and a vocabulary section with words in order of appearance.

Accompanying cassettes are also available to teach correct pronunciation without repetition.

288 pages, 5 ½ x 8 ½, 0-87052-055-5, $14.95 paperback, (511)
2 cassettes, 0-87052-060-1, $12.95, (512)

MASTERING ADVANCED FRENCH, book and audio cassettes

This language textbook provides authentic passages from contemporary sources along with extracts from the poetry and prose of earlier writers -all with explanations of more unusual words, phrases, and grammatical features in the passages, and followed by exercises. The accompanying cassette contains all the dialogues and selected exercises, as well as some literary extracts.

348 pages, 5 ½ x 8 ½, 0-7818-0312-8, $14.95 paperback, (41)
2 cassettes, 0-7818-0313-6, $12.95, (54)

Dictionaries

MISTAKABLE FRENCH: FAUX AMIS & KEY WORDS

Phillip Thody & Howard Evans

This book is a dictionary and guide to 1,000 words which look alike in French and English, but have very different meanings indeed. Thus the French term "colon" also means a colonial settler, "patron" can be a dress pattern, and while "impuissant" may mean impotent, "impotent" means crippled. The individual entries also provide the wide social and cultural context with which the words are used in French.

224 pages, 5 ½ x 8 ½, 1,000 entries, 0-7818-0649-1, $12.95 paperback (720)

COMPREHENSIVE BILIGUAL DICTIONARY OF FRENCH PROVERBS

Monique Brezin-Rossignol

Francis Bacon once remarked that the genius, wit and spirit of a nation can be discovered in its proverbs. 6,000 French proverbs in this unique bilingual collection provide an invaluable classroom aid. The proverbs are arranged in alphabetical order in French and in English.

400 pages, 5 x 8, 6,000 entries, 0-7818-0594-5, $24.95 paperback (700)

DICTIONARY OF 1000 FRENCH PROVERBS

Peter Mertvago

Organized alphabetically by key words, this bilingual reference book is a guide to and an information source for a key element of French.

131 pages, 5 x 7, 0-7818-0400-0, $11.95 paperback, (146)

FRENCH-ENGLISH DICTIONARY OF GASTRONOMIC TERMS

B. Luce

Admirers of French cuisine have a real treat for their future travels to France-or a local French restaurant. They can take with them the most comprehensive dictionary of menu terms (over 20,000 of them) prepared by LA MAISON DU DICTIONNAIRE in Paris to help French chefs translate and explain their menus to English speaking visitors. Many definitions are very informative on ingredients and sometimes read like mini-recipes. Armchair travelers and gourmets can join in the feast.

500 pages, 8 ½, 20,000 entries, 0-7818-0555-4, $24.95 paperback (655)

French Interest Titles for Children

Hippocrene Children's Illustrated Bilingual Dictionary
ENGLISH-FRENCH/FRENCH-ENGLISH

The earlier a child gains a basic knowledge of a language, the easier it will be master to the language later. Now children have this enticing dictionary to prepare them for French classes in school, providing them with 500 basic words together with large illustrations.

96 pages, 8 ½ x 11, ISBN 0-7818-0710-7, $14.95 hardcover (797)

500 REALLY USEFUL FRENCH WORDS AND PHRASES FOR CHILDREN

Carol Watson and Philippa Moyle,
illustrated by Teresa Foster

This colorful book is a simple and useful guide to the French language. Young students will find out what life is like for the French Flaubert family dining out, going shopping, on a camping trip, making friends, or visiting new places. There are instructive pronunciation guides and useful everyday phrases to introduce the language to young readers, aged 10 and up.

32 pages, 8 x 10, full color illustrations, 0-7818-0267-9, $8.95 hardcover (37)

TALES OF LANGUEDOC FROM THE SOUTH OF FRANCE
Samuel Jacques Brun

For children to older adults (and everyone in between), here is a masterful collection of folk tales from the south of France.

Ages 12 and up

248 pages, 33 b/w sketches, 5 ½ x 8 ¼, 0-7818-0715-8, $14.95 hardcover, (793)

French Love Poetry

CLASSIC FRENCH LOVE POEMS
edited by Lisa Neal

This book contains 77 inspiring French poems in English translation, including a complete translation of Paul Géraldy's *Toi et Moi*. Among other authors included are Charles Baudelaire, Arthur Rimbaud, Marie de France, Victor Hugo, and Guy de Maupassant. The text is accompanied by 25 beautiful illustrations by famous artist Maurice LeLoir.

130 pages, 6 x 9, 25 illustrations, 0-7818-0573-4, $17.50 hardcover (672)

TREASURY OF CLASSIC FRENCH LOVE SHORT STORIES, BILINGUAL
edited and translated by Lisa Neal

10 short stories span eight centuries of French literature. Nine celebrated French writers are represented: Marie de France, Margueritte de Navarre, Madame de Lafayette, Guy de Maupassant, Rétif de la Bretonne, Alphonse Daudet, Auguste de Villiers de l'Isle, Gabrielle-Sidonie Colette, and Jean Giono. The text includes the original French with side by side English translation.

128 pages, 5 x 7, 0-7818-0511-2, $11.95 hardcover (621)

TREASURY OF FRENCH LOVE POEMS, QUOTATIONS, AND PROVERBS, BILINGUAL
edited and translated by Richard A. Branyon. Also available on cassette

This collection of French love poems, quotations and proverbs reflects a culture deeply affected by the affairs of the heart. Subjects such as lust, betrayal, true love, marriage, and obsession are explored in 25 poems and over 100 proverbs and quotations. The text includes the original French with side by side translation.

128 pages, 5 x 7, 0-7818-0307-1, $11.95 hardcover (344)
cassettes: 0-7818-0359-4, $12.95 (580) 120 minutes